Inclusive
Games

Susan L. Kasser, MS
Oregon State University

Human Kinetics

Library of Congress Cataloging-in-Publication Data

Kasser, Susan L.
  Inclusive games / Susan L. Kasser.
    p. cm.
  Includes bibliographical references.
  ISBN 0-87322-639-9 (pbk.)
  1. Sports for children. 2. Games. I. Title.
  GV709.2.K38 1995
  796'.01922--dc20   95-17902
                                                                    CIP

ISBN: 0-87322-639-9
Copyright © 1995 by Susan L. Kasser

Acquisitions Editors: Scott Wikgren and Rick Frey; **Developmental Editors:** Glennda Kouts and Elaine Mustain; **Assistant Editors:** Erin Cler, Ed Giles, Susan Moore, John Wentworth; **Editorial Assistant:** Andrew Starr; **Copyeditor:** David Frattini; **Proofreader:** Julia Anderson; **Typesetter and Layout Artist:** Kathy Boudreau-Fuoss and Tara Welsch; **Text Designer:** Stuart Cartwright; **Photo Editor:** Boyd La Foon; **Cover Designer:** Jack Davis; **Photographers (interior):** Dee Damkoehler (pp. 5,19,41,99) and Doug Collier (p. 75); **Illustrator:** Mary Yemma Long; **Printer:** United Graphics

Human Kinetics books are available at special discounts for bulk purchase. Special editions or book excerpts can also be created to specification. For details, contact the Special Sales Manager at Human Kinetics.

Printed in the United States of America   10   9   8   7   6   5   4   3   2

Human Kinetics
Web site: http://www.humankinetics.com/

United States: Human Kinetics, P.O. Box 5076, Champaign, IL 61825-5076
1-800-747-4457
e-mail: humank@hkusa.com

Canada: Human Kinetics, Box 24040, Windsor, ON N8Y 4Y9
1-800-465-7301 (in Canada only)
e-mail: humank@hkcanada.com

Europe: Human Kinetics, P.O. Box IW14, Leeds LS16 6TR, United Kingdom
(44) 1132 781708
e-mail: humank@hkeurope.com

Australia: Human Kinetics, 57A Price Avenue, Lower Mitcham, South Australia 5062
(08) 277 1555
e-mail: humank@hkaustralia.com

New Zealand: Human Kinetics, P.O. Box 105-231, Auckland 1
(09) 523 3462
e-mail: humank@hknewz.com

To my students at Metcalf School, whose excitement and zest for movement motivated me to create and explore an endless possibility of games and activities; the staff at Metcalf, who allowed me the opportunity to develop and grow as a professional; and to my family and friends, whose support and encouragement led the way. Thank you!

CONTENTS

PREFACE

Excitement fills the gym. Children are running this way and that. Starting, stopping, and starting again. Some are darting to the right, others dodging to the left. A few are skipping, some are spinning, others leaping. Giggling and laughter abound.

One boy runs after another. He reaches out but misses. He turns and sprints toward another in the group, but the distance grows between them. He runs after another, but cannot catch him. He tries again and again without success. Finally, he just stops running. A girl, who was tagged first, watches from the side of the gym; her crutch tips barely touch the line that separates her world from that of her friends.

This scene is often typical of an elementary gym class.

What happened to that kindergartner whose eyes used to gleam when he heard it was time for PE? What happened to that sheer excitement he used to have as he headed for the gym? Not long ago it took everything he had to contain the energy surging through his body. Back then, the gym was magical. It was where creativity, imagination, and excitement came together. This child was excited about life. He wanted to experience everything! What happened to his zest for movement? Where did the discoveries he was so eager to uncover in gym class lead him?

Unfortunately, PE classes lead many children to discover simply that they are not as good as their peers. They find that they cannot throw, catch, or run as well as many other girls and boys. Their confidence disappears and they learn to shy away from new experiences. They learn to dislike physical activity.

Why does this happen to these youngsters? Perhaps it's because we teach those with physical differences that they cannot play in the same games as their friends; or maybe it's because we teach children that they must all fit into the same mold. We seem to forget their individuality and to look at them all as one group to be taught the same activity in the same way with the same rules. We expect them all to perform exactly alike. This impossible expectation steals their zest and excitement for movement.

Even though our intentions are good, we often lack the training and expertise necessary to modify activities to meet the unique abilities of all those involved. Wouldn't it be wonderful if we could put the magic of activity back into their hearts?

This book does just that. It provides practical suggestions and concrete examples for both regular and adapted physical educators who want to make their programs inclusive as well as optimal for all children.

The book begins with information on planning and developing games, and it provides general guidelines for individualizing activities for all participants. The following chapters offer games and activities for all developmental levels. The descriptions and details regarding adaptations or modifications will enable you to take specific motor differences and abilities into account as you use the games.

In the pages that follow, you will improve your ability to include all children at their individual levels. You will learn to help each child succeed in physical activity and to enhance each child's self-worth. You will discover how to provide an atmosphere in which each child can, once again, discover the magic of movement.

The first chapter discusses why it is essential to include all children—regardless of ability—in movement games. The strategies chapter 1 develops can be applied to any game or activity, in a variety of situations, and with all children.

Although the games in the last four chapters are grouped by chronological age, it is important for you to recognize that chronological age and functional ability often differ. Chronological age may often be a poor indicator of a child's physical abilities. In planning and using inclusive activities, you must consider the interplay between functional and chronological age to select appropriate games. Some first graders, for example, can easily complete activities designated for the third grade; conversely, some third graders may be hard pressed to do activities that younger children easily accomplish. The key is to select age-appropriate activities which are then modified to meet individual functional abilities.

Children love to be active and to be challenged with respect to their physical abilities, especially if this challenge offers them success and enjoyment. The attitudes demonstrated by the flexible and accepting teacher who gives every child this opportunity will filter down to all the students. You can use the many strategies for modifying activities in *Inclusive Games* to become that kind of effective teacher and positive role model. As the physical educator, you can foster both self-acceptance and respect for others within each child by including each one as part of the group.

GAME FINDER

Key to Chapters

Chapter 2 = Preschool Activities
Chapter 3 = Primary Activities: Kindergarten to Grade Three
Chapter 4 = Advanced Activities: Grades Four through Six
Chapter 5 = Adapted Sport Activities: Grades Six and Above

Key to Difficulty

Easy =
Medium =
Complex =

Game/Skills	Chapter	Difficulty	Players	Page
Across the Great Divide Cooperation; Communication	4		6 or more	90
Airplane Fly Crossing midline; Balances	2		8-10	20
Apple Picking Locomotor skills; Underhand throwing	2		Any	27
Baseball Batting; Fielding; Base running	5		8-10/team	102
Beams and Ladders Balance; Fitness; Jumping	2		Any	34
Body Bowling Log rolling	2		Any	21
Bulldozer Blast Locomotor skills; Back strength	2		Any	36
Car Rally Locomotor skills; Agility	3		Any	42
Centipede Throwing; Running; Dodging	4		4 or more	76
Chocolate Chip Cookies Locomotor skills	2		Any	28

Game/Skills	Chapter	Difficulty	Players	Page
Mission Possible Soccer skills	4		3-7/group	78
Mystery Search Locomotor skills; Balances	2		Any	30
Ninja Turtles Locomotor skills	3		6 or more	44
Octopus Tag Locomotor skills; Dodging; Tagging	3		6 or more	54
Peanut Butter and Jelly Locomotor skills	3		6 or more	45
Pin Ball Throwing	4		2 or more	80
Poison Ball Overhand throwing	3		8 or more	46
Poison Peanut Butter Pit Cooperation; Communication	4		8 or more	95
Ponies in the Barn Throwing, Galloping; Agility	3		6 or more	70
Popcorn Locomotor skills; Underhand throwing	2		Any	24
Puppy Dog Tails Locomotor skills; Eye-foot coordination	3		4 or more	56
Rolling Red Light Kicking; Soccer skills	3		Any	58
Roll Over Throwing	3		4 or more	72
Ship Ahoy! Locomotor skills; Fitness	3		Any	47
Skittleball Eye-hand coordination	3		6-8/station	48
Square Off Throwing	4		4 or more	87
Steal the Bacon Running; Throwing; Catching	3		6 or more	60
Sticky Marshmallow Prone weight shifting; Head/back extension	2		8-10	25

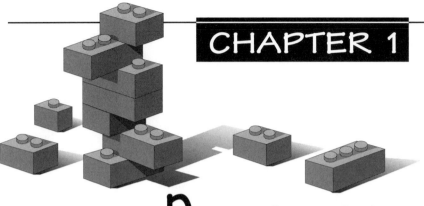

CHAPTER 1

DEVELOPING AND INDIVIDUALIZING GAMES

Games were meant to be played, not watched from a distance. While watching games does offer a few vicarious benefits, these benefits cannot compare with the excitement of actual participation.

 # How Valuable Are Games?

Think back to when you were young. Remember how exciting it was to chase a ball, roll down a hill, or run after a playmate in the schoolyard? With these vivid images in your head, you will most likely agree that movement offers much to the life of a child. Physical activity and the experience of developing one's body and skills offer desirable outcomes physically, psychologically, socially, and emotionally for all those who participate.

Movement Games Mean Fun

The sheer enjoyment and pleasure that come from playing in a game are unmistakable. Although moving in and of itself is captivating, games are more motivating and fun than practicing isolated skills. When movement games are played with an emphasis on participation rather than performance, they provide an avenue for all children to express their spirits in dynamic ways.

Movement Games Mean Physical Improvement

Children receive many physical benefits from participating in active games. They are motivated to move, and the increased activity level fosters improved cardiovascular endurance, muscular strength and endurance, flexibility, and body composition. Movement games complement specific, and somewhat more stationary, skill practice. A child's physical maturation will, of course, have an important effect on the child's ability to develop new skills. Games, however, allow the child to improve motor coordination through continued practice in a variety of contexts and situations.

Movement Games Mean Interaction

Although the aforementioned physical benefits are important, they are not first in the hearts and minds of children. The interactive nature of games attracts them. Peer acceptance and a sense of belonging are priorities for these youngsters. Interestingly enough, children often form relationships and make decisions concerning who they will accept into their circle of friends based on appearance and physical skills such as those demonstrated in games. Inclusive games, therefore, offer a supportive environment that enhances each child's self-confidence, regardless of physical ability. Inclusive games can teach children how to succeed, how to accept the strengths and limitations of everyone involved, and how to strive for improvement.

 ## Why Inclusive Games?

Many schoolchildren whose intellectual, physical, emotional, and behavioral characteristics differ markedly from those of their peers require special assistance to realize their potential. Depending upon how drastically their physical capabilities differ, this assistance may or may not include physical education services.

There are many more children, however, whose movement differences are not severe enough to require specialized programs. Instead, they differ enough to warrant consideration within the regular physical education program. These youngsters may be obese, they may be less skilled or lack coordination, or they may simply be less experienced than the others in the group. Any physical education program should foster movement that respects the uniqueness of each individual. In essence, all physical education programs, whether serving regular or special education students, should be adapted physical education—adapted to meet each child's needs, strengths, and abilities.

Children with movement differences have the same desires, interests, and expectations to belong and achieve as their more skilled peers. These children must be given access to physical activities and games through the use of modified equipment, adapted rules, and creative programming; they should receive the same benefits offered other youngsters their age.

Key Programming Principles

When you develop a new game or modify an already existing game to accommodate children with differing abilities, it is important to remember a few basic principles. No matter how creative a game may be or how good the modifications may seem, if the activity does not meet the children's needs, your planning has been in vain, and you will not be using the players' time effectively.

The MAGIC Principles

Think back to the kindergartner with the gleam in his eyes whose imagination and zest made the gym seem magical. By using the MAGIC principles, games and activities will become magical for all your students, whatever their ages and abilities.

M	=	Motivational
A	=	Age-Appropriate
G	=	Growth Oriented
I	=	Individualized
C	=	Comparable

Motivational

Children will be motivated to participate if there is a variety of activities and if the activities emphasize the game itself rather than the development of specific skills. Activities must be fun. Motivated students are more likely to maintain high interest levels. When students are excited about the activities, they are more likely to learn and improve their performance.

Age-Appropriate

Activities must focus on the chronological ages of the children before addressing their functional ages. For example, a juniorhigh student with a physical disability should be afforded the opportunity to learn and play in a modified football game and not merely offered wheelchair obstacle courses or throwing to targets. Thoughtful programming allows the development of age-appropriate skills and affords children—who see what others their age are doing—enhanced self-esteem through participation in appropriate activity.

Growth Oriented

All education attempts to promote growth and skill development. To achieve this end, activities must be modified only as much as necessary to afford success while still allowing a challenge. If activities are too easy, students are likely to become bored and unmotivated. Progress can be slowed or stopped altogether. Success and challenge must be continually balanced throughout the program.

Individualized

Activities that target the ability levels of all those involved help players feel better about their participation within the group. They are less likely to sit out if it is clear to them that they are a significant part of the game. Inclusion is the important theme to remember. Individualization does not suggest separate lesson plans for each child, nor does it suggest designing different activities within the same class for different children. Individualization will be successful with much simpler changes to your program.

Comparable

Participation in physical education and activity programming must be comparable for children of all skill levels and abilities. Less-skilled players should not be assigned only as the scorekeeper or as the turner for the jump rope. Instead, they should have opportunities to develop the skills that would allow them to play a variety of positions or share in many aspects of the activity.

Curricular Principles

Once you have considered these MAGIC principles, it is important to think about the curricular emphasis of programming. Plan and select games or activities based on the skills players should achieve as a result of their participation. The types of games that will be offered and the order in which they will be played are extremely important. The basic considerations in all movement activities include safety, group size, and purpose. For inclusive games, however, ages and specific ability levels become priorities.

Age

As children develop, they progress through a series of developmental movement patterns and skills (Figure 1.1). What differs among children is the timing and facility with which they move along this continuum. The following are three characteristics of typical motor development:

1. Development is, for the most part, sequential. It occurs in a mostly fixed sequence, depending upon a variety of factors and contexts. These fundamental movement patterns lay the foundation for more complex motor skills as the child ages.

2. Development has overlapping stages. A child's movements are not exclusively in any one particular stage at a time. She may demonstrate components of one stage while simultaneously exhibiting beginning components of the next level.

3. Development builds on previous skills. Should the demands of a specific task be more difficult or complex than the child can master, the child may revert to an earlier stage in which he is more secure and confident.

If we understand and accept that all children develop differently, then we must also understand the need to program differently for different youngsters. After children learn basic movements within the context of their own bodies, they begin to integrate the movements with one another and with other variables. We need to help children follow this progression according to their unique developmental patterns. When children first

a. Prone with head extension   b. Prone on elbows

e. Rolling over   f. Prone extended arm support

i. Four-point or all-fours stance   j. Creeping

m. Cruising   n. Standing

Figure 1.1   Sequence of developmental movement patterns.

c. Rocking side to side   d. Rolling from prone to supine

g. Crossing midline   h. Crawling (on belly)

k. Kneeling   l. Half-kneeling

o. Walking

enter school they build on this foundation of movement by incorporating basic motor skills. Programming for children at this age focuses on the following individual, closed (noninteractive) skills.

Locomotor	Manipulative	Movement Exploration
Rolling	Catching	Body Awareness
Crawling	Throwing	Balance and Stunt Activities
Running	Rolling	Rhythms
Galloping	Bouncing	Simple Games
Jumping	Striking	
Hopping	Kicking	
Skipping		

Fourth- through sixth-grade programming emphasizes the use of these basic skills within open or interactive situations. Skills are now developed and practiced in variable contexts established by other individuals or the total group. Programming shifts to afford experience within this interactive environment using activities such as

- Physical fitness
- Gymnastic activities
- Rhythms and dance
- Dual and dynamic manipulative skills
- Lead-up games to individual and team sports

Ability

Most children follow a specified progression in the development of individual movements and skills. A natural progression occurs from the simple to the more complex (Table 1.1). Where children are along this continuum at any given time varies, whether or not they are identified as having a disability. Games, therefore, must be designed to permit variety and be flexible enough to allow progressions within a particular activity to occur.

Table 1.1   Motor Skill Progressions

Skill	Progression
Running	Runs randomly, follows course or direction, follows course through obstacles, evades field of stationary objects, evades field of moving objects or others.
Jumping	Jumps up/down, jumps forward, jumps forward varying distances, jumps down from height, jumps up to height.
Galloping	Runs with uneven rhythm, moves forward using same lead foot/trunk sideways, moves forward using same lead foot/trunk forward, gallops with consistent rhythm.
Hopping	One foot to two foot landing, hops up/down with support, hops up/down, hops forward, hops down from height, hops up to height.
Skipping	Runs, gallops, leaps; same side skip; segmented alternate skip; skips consistent pattern, irregular rhythm; skips rhythmically.
Bouncing	Bounces away from self, bounces and catches, bounces continuously using same hand, bounces continuously alternating hands.
Kicking	Kicks stationary ball, kicks slow rolling ball, kicks fast rolling ball, kicks with moving or rapid approach.
Striking	Strikes stationary ball, strikes slow rolling ball, strikes suspended ball swinging in arc, strikes slowly tossed ball.
Catching	Catches rolled ball, catches ball swinging in arc, catches slowly tossed ball to midline, moves to catch ball.
Throwing	Throws forward to stationary target, forward to target slowly moving across field, forward to target moving randomly in area.
Dynamic balance	Sitting; kneeling; half-kneeling; static one foot; one foot on, one off; standing sideways; side stepping; standing forward; same foot leading; alternate stepping.

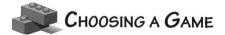 Modifying Games

Although there is no single, specific way to individualize for everyone, here are some guidelines that may be helpful:

1. Establish where in the developmental continuum the child functions.

2. Analyze the elements of the activity, and design a progression of steps to accomplish the task.

3. Identify the elements of the game or activity that could be changed, and alter them based upon individual needs.

   • **Equipment**. Change the weight and size of objects and implements, target size, and ball resiliency.

   • **Space**. Change the space involved in the activity, such as the distance from the target, the height of the target, or the number of yards between bases.

   • **Time**. Vary the time it takes to complete an activity or the number of repetitions.

   • **Force**. Alter the force or speed required for an activity. Slow the activity down, or substitute stationary tasks for moving ones.

   • **Rules and Responsibilities**. Simplify expectations for different individuals. Eliminate rules, reduce the choices available, or eliminate quick changes in roles.

4. Change the element only as much as necessary to afford success, but preserve the challenge for each individual. Elements can be altered for different individuals within the same game.

5. Adapt already existing games. Do not always create new ones.

6. Repeat the same game, but use different skills or equipment.

7. Individualize elements as play continues to ensure ongoing success.

8. Ensure that adaptations are age-appropriate.

9. Avoid bringing down the level of the entire class to that of the one or two children who are less skilled. Doing so only creates a negative attitude in the rest of the students toward those children; it also ignores and defeats the practice of individualization for the higher-skilled children.

Choosing a Game

Many games are typically geared to the highly skilled students in the class. Make games more inclusive by

1. presenting them sequentially, beginning with games that require the simplest level of a skill and following them with games involving more complex skills and interactions;

2. using them within a unit to complement isolated skill practice and drills;

3. organizing them to provide maximum participation for less-skilled children;

4. suiting them to the age and developmental levels of participants; and

5. adapting them in whatever ways are necessary to meet the needs and abilities of all children involved.

After choosing a game and considering its appropriateness, take time to evaluate the game and its potential effectiveness by answering the following questions:

1. Will all children receive a sufficient amount of activity in the game?

2. Will all children feel successful and good about themselves as a result of their involvement?

3. Will all children be appropriately challenged?

4. Will all children be motivated to continue participating and playing in the game?

Using This Book

The activities in the following chapters are presented along the previously described motor development continuum. Chapter 2 focuses on developmental activities and games for the preschooler. Chapter 3 provides games and activities that emphasize the basic motor skills appropriate for children ages five to eight within the primary grades. Chapter 4 involves advanced games and lead-up activities for children in fourth through sixth grades. Chapter 5 provides modifications of specific sports that can be used for students sixth-grade and older.

The activities and games offered here are examples of how a game can be changed to meet the needs and skill levels of all those involved. They may be used, as described, for groups within an adapted physical education class or small groups within the regular physical education program. More importantly, specific adaptations and suggestions may be taken from a given game and used within the framework of another game. In this case, specific adaptations could be used for an individual mainstreamed within the regular physical education program or for a regular education student functioning at a lower motor level than the others in the class.

Use the Organization of the Book to Help You Sequence Activities

Within each chapter, the games are organized and sequenced into three groups according to the difficulty level of the skills involved: easy, moderate, and complex. The logo at the top of each page provides a quick, visual identification of whether the game requires an easy ( ),

moderate ( ), or complex ( ) level of skills. The Game Finder (pp. 1-4) will enable you to locate games quickly by what skills are needed, the developmental level involved (indicated by Key to Chapters), the difficulty within that developmental level, and the number of children who can participate. For a complete list of skills, refer to the game itself.

Study Each Game Carefully to Be Sure You Can Present It Clearly

The following information is provided about each game:

- Number of players
- Equipment needed
- Area recommended
- Skills emphasized
- Description of game or activity
- Theme variations of the activity
- Adaptations for various abilities

For those of you without adapted physical education experience, some of the terminology used in the games may be unfamiliar. The Glossary of Movements and Positions (pp. 109-110) presents definitions of many of these terms.

Variations of the game relate to changes in the game's theme or concept, particular skill used, number of teams, or cooperative versus competitive organization. Adaptations of the activity are suggested specifically for the ability levels of individuals within the game and refer to modifications in distances, target sizes, skill, equipment, or rules.

The challenge for each physical educator is to provide a creative and flexible program that is adaptable and includes all students. After trying some of the games in this book and experimenting with the accompanying modifications, you should begin to understand the concepts of individualization and inclusion, and you should begin to feel more comfortable with game adaptations. There may be occasions where only slight modifications are necessary, or there may be times when major changes in game elements are required to meet the diverse abilities, needs, and interests of participants within the group. In any case, you can make games inclusive for all children and bring the magic of activity back to each of them.

CHAPTER 2

PRESCHOOL ACTIVITIES

Airplane Fly

Players:	8 to 10
Equipment:	A long rope, six whiffle balls, two chairs, and airplane cutouts
Area:	Classroom or gymnasium
Skills:	Prone on elbows, sitting balance, kneeling balance, crossing midline (refer to Figure 1.1 on pages 10 and 11)
Activity:	Arrange players in various positions, side by side and in a line. Attach a cutout of an airplane to the side of each whiffle ball. String a long rope through each whiffle ball and secure it on both ends to two chairs; make the rope taut. Players make the "airplane" fly by reaching for the ball with an open palm and pushing it laterally to the next person in line. Each player pushes the ball along the rope until all airplanes have flown from one "airport" (chair) to the other.
Variation:	• Use various vehicle cutouts such as cars, bicycles, or boats, or try holiday items such as ghosts, turkeys, or reindeer.
Adaptations:	• Use deck tennis rings instead of whiffle balls to afford a larger contact surface or an object to grasp.
	• Manually adjust the height of the rope as it passes by each student to accommodate the various heights and positions of the participants.

Body Bowling

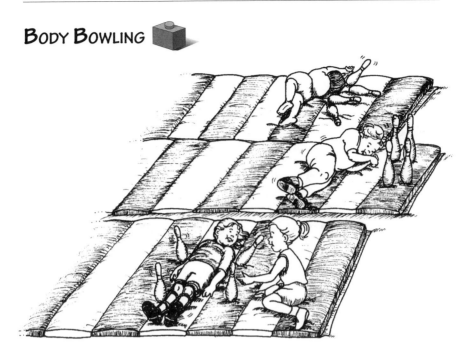

Players:	Any number
Equipment:	Mats and plastic bowling pins
Area:	Classroom or gymnasium
Skill:	Log rolling
Activity:	Set up plastic pins at the end of each mat. Each player lies supine on one end of the mat, across from a set of pins. Tell players they are big, colorful bowling balls. Each ball log rolls the distance of the mat and knocks over the pins at the other end.
Variations:	• Have another child act as the bowling pin and stand at the end of the mat. When touched by the "ball" the second child falls down like a pin. Some "pins" may even wobble but not fall down.
	• Use 10 players to act as a set of pins.
	• Use various locomotor skills instead of log rolling.
Adaptations:	• Vary the distance to the pins for less-skilled rollers.
	• For a child unable to roll, set the pins beside the child and have the ball rock from side to side.
	• Encourage range of motion by having a child unable to rock reach out to knock over the pins.

DOUGHNUT DELIVERY

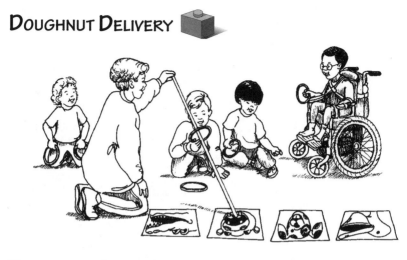

Players: Any number

Equipment: Deck tennis rings, long dowel or wand, and animal pictures

Area: Classroom or gymnasium

Skills: Upper-extremity range of motion, sitting, upper-extremity strength

Activity: Position players sitting side by side in a line. Spread out large pictures of various animals in front of the children and tell them that the animals came to school without breakfast and are hungry. A child feeds the animals by reaching up and putting a "doughnut" (deck tennis ring) on the end of a wooden wand that the instructor holds and angles down to the animal picture on the floor. The child lets go of the doughnut and watches it slide down the wand to feed the animals. The instructor moves down the line to each child and repeats the same process until all have had a turn.

Variations: • Feed the animals Spaghettios.

                   • Use balls on a ramp to feed the animals gumdrops or meatballs.

Adaptations: • Vary the positions of children to achieve individual objectives such as sitting balance, four-point stance, prone on elbows with weight shift, or kneeling balance.

                   • Vary the height of the wand's end nearest the child to foster an optimal range of motion.

                   • Have children cross the midline to put the doughnut on the wand.

Hot Dog!

Players: Two per group, as many groups as needed

Equipment: One towel or blanket per group

Area: Classroom or gymnasium

Skills: Log rolling, knee walking, creeping, seal walking

Activity: Spread flat a towel or blanket. One child lies down at one end of the blanket, positioned so that the head, neck, and shoulders are off the blanket. This child begins to log roll across the length of the blanket. A partner ensures that the blanket wraps around the rolling child. The child continues log rolling, while the partner knee walks or creeps beside until the "hot dog" is wrapped tight in the roll. The partner pretends to put ketchup and mustard on the hot dog. Have the child unroll, and allow the players to switch places and repeat the game.

Variation: • Make wrapped candy or burritos instead of hot dogs.

Adaptations: • Have the child roll down a wedge bolster if initiation of trunk rotation and rolling on a flat surface is difficult.

• If increased strength of trunk rotators is desired, use a wedge bolster to have the child roll up.

• Vary the length of the blanket based on individual abilities to roll.

POPCORN

Players: Any number

Equipment: Yarn balls

Area: Gymnasium

Skills: Locomotor skills, underhand throwing, agility or body awareness

Activity: Scatter yarn balls randomly throughout the playing area. Players are then instructed to move around the room but not to touch any of the popcorn kernels while the oil heats up. When given the "pop" cue, each player begins picking up balls, one at a time, and underhand tossing them toward the ceiling. Each player pops a piece of popcorn, shouting out "Pop!" with each toss. After each "pop," the child moves on to another piece. Soon, all are involved in popping the popcorn and the room is full of action. Stop players after a designated time period.

Variation: • Pretend the balls are snowballs. Have students pretend to make and pack the snowball before tossing it into the air.

Adaptation: • For students using wheelchairs and unable to reach the floor, have yarn balls already placed in their laps. Require these students to pop the balls from their laps and move to another spot before popping other pieces.

STICKY MARSHMALLOW

Players:	8 to 10
Equipment:	A large, 16-inch beach ball
Area:	Classroom or gymnasium
Skills:	Prone on elbows with weight shifting, head and back extension, range of motion
Activity:	Position players on their stomachs, in a circle with their heads toward the center. Assure that there is adequate room in the center for the ball to move. Each player must push the large beach ball away and toward someone else in the circle. Instruct players to use one or two hands, depending upon individual objectives. Each child tries to ensure that the "sticky marshmallow" does not touch the top of the head or face to avoid being covered with a sticky mess.
Variations:	• Have more than one ball in motion at a time.
	• Have students catch the ball with two hands and then push it away.
Adaptations:	• Deflate the beach ball slightly to decrease the ball's speed and bounce; do not let the ball become so deflated that it dampens excitement in the game.
	• Use balls of various sizes.
	• Decrease the distance between players for those with limited strength or range of motion.

TURKEY PLUCK

Players: Six to eight

Equipment: Six to eight flag-football flags and one flag-football belt

Area: Classroom or gymnasium

Skills: Prone on elbows, sitting balance, kneeling balance, range of motion

Activity: Position players in either a prone, sitting, half-kneeling, or kneeling position side by side in a line. Place flags on the velcro portion of the belt to resemble tail feathers. Place the belt around your waist. Tell the players that the flags are turkey feathers and that they all must help pluck the turkey. Move slowly across the group, allowing each player to reach up and pull off one of the feathers. The game continues until all the players have had a chance to pluck three or four feathers.

Variations:
- Hold the belt, and have the players reach up and put flags on it to make a beautiful headdress.
- Have students work on jumping skills by wearing the velcro belt up high on your body.

Adaptations:
- Move more slowly to allow each student time to pull the feathers.
- Fasten flags less securely to the belt for children with limited strength.
- If grasping is a problem, allow the student to put a fist down on the end of the flag and hold it against the floor while you move forward to detach the flag.

Apple Picking

Players: Any number

Equipment: Tree targets, yarn balls, tape, and large crates or boxes

Area: Gymnasium

Skills: Locomotor skills, underhand throwing

Activity: Place large pictures of trees on the wall at one end of the playing area. Randomly tape yarn balls on these trees to simulate apples. Large crates or boxes are placed at the other end of the playing area. Players are instructed to move across the area to the trees, pick off one of the apples, return to the other side, and underhand throw the apples into the boxes. Players continue in this fashion until all the apples have been picked.

Variation: • Vary the type of fruit being picked.

Adaptations: • Vary the heights of the fruit for students with limited range of motion.

• Modify the distance specific individuals must travel to the trees according to their mobility and speed.

• Have students remain stationary and perform balances (kneeling, half-kneeling, or prone with extended forearm support) while reaching for apples.

• Alter the distance students must throw the apples into the boxes, or have students who are unable to throw balls drop them into the boxes.

CHOCOLATE CHIP COOKIES

Players: Any number

Equipment: Beanbags and one hoop for each child

Area: Gymnasium

Skills: Locomotor skills

Activity: Spread hoops on one side of the playing area. Each child is positioned across from the hoops and given a handful of beanbags. The children are told that they will be making chocolate chip cookies by putting the chips in plain cookies across the way. Children shuttle back and forth using various locomotor skills to drop chips into the cookies one at a time. When all the chocolate chips have been used, have the group count the chips in each of the cookies.

Variations: • Use colored beanbags as M & M's for the cookies.

• Make a pizza with many toppings.

Adaptations: • Based on individual abilities, utilize various locomotor skills such as log rolling, knee walking, jumping, or galloping.

• Vary distances specific children must travel to make cookies so that all end at about the same time with an equal number of chips.

• Have children do various animal walks, such as the seal walk or crab walk, in order to work on prefitness goals.

• Have children throw bags into hoops from varying distances.

Clown Face

Players: Any number

Equipment: Tape and a clown's face with eyes, nose, ears, and mouth cutouts (one set for each one or two players)

Area: Gymnasium

Skills: Locomotor skills, balances, range of motion

Activity: Place clown face targets on the wall across from the players. Secure tape on these targets where specific features, such as the eyes and ears, will be placed. Give each player a specific facial part. Ask the player to move across the area, adhere the part to the appropriate space on the clown's face, and return for the next piece. Players continue in this fashion until all the parts have been adhered and the clown's face is complete.

Variations: • Use barn targets and farm animal cutouts.

                • Use a basket and pieces of fruit.

Adaptations: • Vary the players' locomotor movements in accordance with individual objectives.

                • Have the players remain stationary just ahead of the target in specific balance positions such as kneeling or half-kneeling. Players reach up to place the cutouts on the target.

                • Vary the height of the clown targets, or have students with limited range of motion put on the lower pieces while other students put on higher pieces.

                • Modify the distance individual players must travel to the targets according to their mobility and speed.

Mystery Search

Players:	Any number
Equipment:	Spot markers or bases and laminated numbers
Area:	Gymnasium
Skills:	Locomotor skills, balances
Activity:	Randomly scatter spot markers on the floor throughout the playing area. Under each marker, hide a different number. Instruct the players to move around the area until given a cue to stop and perform a specific skill. Each player then picks up one marker, looks to see what number is hidden underneath, and performs the specified movement or skill in accordance with the number uncovered. Vary the locomotor movements players use to travel around the

area and the skill each performs when given cues to stop. Players can hop, jump up and down, or stand on one foot for each of the different numbers found under the markers. After completing the movement, players cover the number with the spot marker before traveling on.

Variations:
- Use letters under the markers, and have students identify the letters or shape their bodies to match the letter.
- Use animal pictures under the markers, and have students both move like that animal and make the appropriate sound.

Adaptations:
- Have students who are nonambulatory perform claps, log rolls, arm lifts for range of motion, or wheelchair push-ups.
- For students unable to reach the floor, supply a plastic bat or reaching implement to allow them to slide the marker off the hidden number. You may need to provide assistance to replace the markers.
- Request specific fitness exercises such as sit-ups or jumping jacks at each marker.

ICE CREAM CONE CREATORS

Players: Any number

Equipment: Four smooth ropes, scooters, beanbags, hoops, and tape

Area: Gymnasium

Skills: Arm strength, leg strength, underhand throwing

Activity: Stretch out each rope lengthwise across the playing area and secure at both ends. Leave adequate space between each rope length. Place colored beanbags in piles and scooters at one end of each rope. At the other end of each rope, place a hoop on the floor with tape extending out in the shape of a cone. These are the ice cream cones. Players pick up one bean bag, lie on their backs on the scooters, place the bean bag on their stomachs, and pull hand over hand along the rope. Once at the ice cream cone, the players get off the scooters, stand up, and underhand throw the beanbags into the cones to add sprinkles or toppings. Players then sit on the scooters and use their legs to return to the pile of beanbags. Assure that each player travels back away from the rope and others who are moving toward the cones. Players shuttle back and forth in this fashion until all ice cream cones have been decorated.

Variations:
- Have children work on color identification by requiring only green sprinkles on one cone, yellow on another, and so on.
- Have beanbags represent cereal to be put in bowls.

Adaptations:
- For students with increased arm strength, use carpet squares instead of scooters.
- Have students with increased spasticity and limited range of motion push along the rope instead of pulling along it.
- Have students in wheelchairs do the activity in their wheelchairs, and provide assistance for positioning and straight direction.
- Use adapted scooters, or secure students with limited trunk control on scooters with gait belts.

BEAMS AND LADDERS

Players: Any number

Equipment: Spot markers or carpet squares, balance beams or boards, flat ladders, box dice, and task cards

Area: Gymnasium

Skills: Balance, jumping, eye-foot coordination, physical fitness

Activity: Arrange the playing area as an obstacle course in which there is a path of colored circles with either balance beams or ladders connecting them. Children start by throwing the box dice. A child moves by jumping the designated number of times along the spot markers. Should the child land on a circle that has a ladder extension, the child can move along the ladder up to the spot marker at the end and, in so doing, bypass some of the markers. Should a child land on a circle with a balance beam or board extension, that child must move down the beam to the marker at its end and, in so doing, move back to a previously passed position. Some markers may be designated as spot checks. When reaching these markers, the child must pick a task card from a face-down pile of cards nearby and perform the activity written on the card. The child then remains at that spot, moves ahead, or moves back as indicated by a number and direction written on the card. The game continues until all children reach the end of the course. Have a few children move simultaneously so that students are not waiting too long between turns (use more than one box dice).

Variations:
- Put other obstacles, such as tires or boxes, in the course.
- Incorporate throwing and catching at certain spot checks.

Adaptations:
- Allow students to step to markers, step between the rungs of the ladders, side step on the balance beams, or move across the beam with one foot on the floor.
- Have students in wheelchairs move in and out of cones instead of along the ladders and roll alongside the beams on the floor.
- Modify task cards with various levels of activities, such as three jumping jacks, two squats, or three arm reaches, to accommodate different abilities.

Bulldozer Blast

Players:	Any number
Equipment:	Foam pieces, scooters, and spot markers
Area:	Gymnasium
Skills:	Locomotor skills, shoulder and back strength
Activity:	Give each student a pile of foam pieces. Place a poly spot marker across the playing area from each pile to indicate the site of the soon to be built skyscraper. Each student picks up a piece of foam, travels to a marker, places the foam piece on the marker, and returns to get another "brick." Players continue to shuttle in this manner, stacking foam pieces on top of one another, until the skyscrapers are built. Next, players lie prone on a scooter and become bulldozers. Instruct each child to keep the head up and the arms extended forward with the palms toward the foam stack. Grasp the student's legs and push the child on the scooter toward the skyscraper. The student maintains an extended arm and head position and knocks down the foam stack. Repeat the process as many times as desired.
Variations:	• Have the foam stack represent snow with the students acting as snowplows or represent trees with the students serving as bulldozers.
	• Have the students fly in an airplane through the clouds.

Adaptations:

- Vary the height of the foam stack, depending upon the student's range of motion.

- Vary locomotor movements and distances to the markers for specific students.

- Have the student build the skyscraper while remaining stationary to work on range of motion or specific balances.

- Allow students to maneuver the scooter using alternate hand movements, or have students sit on the scooter and use the legs to propel the scooter.

FEED THE ANIMALS

Players: Two or more

Equipment: Yarn balls, wedge bolster or mats, and benches

Area: Gymnasium

Skills: Eye-hand coordination, locomotor skills, balance positions

Activity: Position half the group at the top of a wedge bolster or ramp made from mats and benches. The remaining players form a line over to one side and at the bottom of the ramp. As a group, these players move across the area at the bottom of the ramp and perform specific animal walks. The animal feeders, at the top, roll yarn balls down the ramp to touch or feed the "animals" moving across. Each time an animal is fed, that animal makes the appropriate animal sound. After this group has moved by and been fed, players switch places and repeat the process.

Variation: • Have cars move across and beep when touched by a ball.

Adaptations: • Have the feeders assume various positions (prone on elbows, kneeling, or half-kneeling) based on individual goals.

- Require animals to make sounds as they move in order to provide verbal cues for those with visual impairments.
- Select the type of animal, such as an entire group of turtles, in order to control speed.

FLYING HIGH

Players: Any number

Equipment: Mats and cylinder bolsters of various circumferences

Area: Gymnasium

Skills: Head, shoulder, and upper-back strength

Activity: Place mats end to end in order to create a long runway. Place cylinder-shaped bolsters of various circumferences side by side, from largest to smallest, at one end of the runway. Be sure to leave some space between the bolsters to allow them to roll. A player lies prone on the first bolster with the head up and arms extended forward. When ready, the player gently pushes off with the legs and begins to move forward. The size, shape, and placement of the bolsters will cause the player to roll forward, thus moving the airplane along the runway. Remind students to keep their heads and arms up until the plane lands. Bolsters must be reset for each student.

Variation: • Have students pretend to be birds or superheroes.

Adaptations: • Use fewer and smaller bolsters for students with limited control.

                 • You may need to assist the bolsters to roll if the student cannot generate enough momentum.

                 • Assist the airplane at the end of the roll by supporting the upper torso and head, if necessary. Others can perform straight arm supports and hand-walk off the last bolster.

CHAPTER 3

PRIMARY
ACTIVITIES

CAR RALLY

Players: Any number

Equipment: Circular spot markers (one for each player), hoops (one for each player), green flag, and red flag

Area: Gymnasium

Skills: Locomotor skills, agility and body awareness

Activity: Scatter hoops randomly throughout the playing area. Give each player a circular spot marker, and have them hold it like a steering wheel. Players begin by standing inside a hoop. Inform the players that, on the green flag, they must drive around without touching anyone or anything. When the red flag is waved, they must find a "garage" (hoop) and park their cars. Players use spot markers to steer and may add car noises, such as revving engines and squealing tires. After each red flag, remove a garage from the playing area. The game continues in this manner with drivers sharing garages until only one garage is left. Remind students to drive carefully and to park their cars slowly. Emphasize that you want to avoid crashes and accidents; you can even use a ticket system. Be creative!

Variations: • Have the students hold hoops horizontally around their waists to simulate space ships.

- Have the students hold their arms out to their sides to be airplanes.
- Ask the students to represent animals by performing animal walks to various barns.

Adaptations:

- Vary the speed the group moves by using a yellow flag to slow things down or by spending less time holding up the green flag.
- Use poly markers or bases for students in wheelchairs, and allow them to enter by rolling on top of the garage. Use enough markers to enlarge the area, and encourage other drivers to share this type of garage.
- Allow the students in wheelchairs to have a steering wheel placed in their laps, leaving their arms free to wheel themselves.

NINJA TURTLES

Players: Six or more

Equipment: None

Area: Gymnasium or outdoor playing area

Skills: Locomotor skills

Activity: Designate each player as either a ninja turtle (e.g., Michelangelo) or as an arch-rival (e.g., Shredder). Everyone begins randomly spread out within the playing area. Signal to begin. Players start moving using the directed locomotor skill. When a ninja turtle meets another ninja turtle, the two give each other a "high five" and say "Cowabunga, Dude!" When a ninja turtle and an arch-rival meet, the two pretend to spar for three repetitions. When two arch-rivals meet, they give an evil laugh and go on their way. Players continue in this manner, meeting as many characters as possible before the activity ends.

Variations: • When two turtles meet, have them perform fitness tasks as if they are in training.

                   • Allow players to choose their own characters and to change characters as often as they would like.

Adaptations: • Designate appropriate locomotor skills based upon individual abilities.

                   • Have individuals unable to perform locomotor tasks remain stationary while others move toward them. Encourage range of motion during high fives or sparring.

Peanut Butter and Jelly

Players:	Six or more
Equipment:	None
Area:	Gymnasium or outdoor playing area
Skills:	Locomotor skills
Activity:	Designate each player as either "peanut butter" or "jelly." Everyone begins spread out in the playing area and, on your signal, starts moving, using a specific locomotor skill. When face to face with another person, each player states the designated word. Should one state "peanut butter" and the other state "jelly," the two hug to make a peanut butter and jelly sandwich. Should the two players state the same word, no sandwich can be made, and each player continues to travel. The object is to make as many peanut butter and jelly sandwiches as possible before the instructor ends the activity.

Variations:

- Have players themselves choose the part of the sandwich that they will be when they meet another classmate.

- Use the words "salt" and "pepper," and have players shake when meeting their opposite.

- Use actions instead of words; compatible acts such as throwing and catching could allow the pair to give each other high fives.

Adaptations:

- Designate appropriate locomotor skills or have children using wheelchairs to wheel forward, backward, or in a zigzag pattern.

- Allow a player unable to self-propel the wheelchair to remain stationary while others move toward that player to carry out their parts. Encourage range of motion during hugs or high fives.

POISON BALL

Players:	Eight or more
Equipment:	Yarn balls (at least 15 to 20)
Area:	Gymnasium
Skill:	Overhand throwing
Activity:	Divide the class into two groups; place one group on one side of the playing area and the other group on the opposite side. Randomly scatter yarn balls evenly between the two groups. Designate a specific colored ball as the poison ball. Neither team wants to end up with this ball on its side. On your signal, all players begin throwing the yarn balls from their side over to the other team's side. Players cannot cross the center line to retrieve any balls. Only balls on their designated side may be picked up and thrown. The object of the game is not only to have less balls in a team's "yard" but also to have the poison ball end up on the opponent's side when you signal "Stop!"

Variations:
- Have more than one poison ball.
- Allow players to cross over and help to clean the other yard at any time.

Adaptations:
- Use ramps to roll balls down for those unable to throw.
- Have a partner retrieve balls for anyone unable to reach the ground.
- Allow certain individuals to throw from the center line or to drop balls over the line.

Ship Ahoy!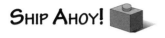

Players:	Any number
Equipment:	None
Area:	Gymnasium
Skills:	Locomotor skills, fitness
Activity:	Instruct players to scatter randomly throughout the playing area. Players begin moving on your signal. As they navigate their own ship, each one tries not to contact, collide, or touch any other ship. Call out various options as the players move: "Hit the deck!"—Players quickly lie on their stomachs. "Submarine!"—Players lie on their backs and lift one leg up in the air to imitate a periscope. "Double submarine!"—Players lie on their backs and lift both legs up for two periscopes. "All's clear!"— Players stand up and resume moving.
Variations:	• Use various locomotor skills.
	• Add different elements (maneuvers) while the players move.
Adaptations:	• Alter the time between calls to adapt the game's pace to the needs of the group.
	• Allow students using wheelchairs to remain in them. Have these students respond to the following commands: "Hit the deck!"—Lean forward. "Submarine!"—Raise one arm in the air. "Double submarine!"—Raise both arms in the air.
	• Allow slower students to respond to your commands at their own speed, even if the pace for others is somewhat faster.

Skittleball

Players: Six to eight (can be used as a station within a circuit)

Equipment: Six to eight suspended ropes with balls at one end, one long rope, and plastic pins

Area: Gymnasium

Skills: Eye-hand coordination, motor planning

Activity: String a long, sturdy rope across the playing area high over the heads of the players. Suspend individual, shorter ropes from this, and attach a ball to the end of each short length. The balls should be suspended just above floor level so that they are able to swing freely. Across from the balls, line up plastic pins side by side. Position a player away from the pins so that when the player releases the suspended ball, it swings and knocks over the pins. Players may move slightly right or left in order to redirect the ball to contact the remaining pins. Players work together to knock over all pins.

Variations: • Use game as a station in a circuit or set up more ropes and pins for additional groups.

- Use targets on a wall instead of pins.
- Assign a specific number of points if the ball hits a hoop taped to the wall.
- Use a stack of foam pieces instead of pins.

Adaptations:
- For students who are nonambulatory, use a shorter rope, and place the pins on a bench. Adjust the rope according to the height of the pins.
- Use larger foam balls or smaller whiffle balls, depending upon the eye-hand coordination and ability of the players.
- Use larger targets or more pins clumped together to increase the target size for less-skilled players.
- Place a foam ball on the lap of a student unable to grasp, and allow the student to push it off.

Toy Soldier

Players:	Two per group (as many groups as needed)
Equipment:	Yarn balls and spot markers
Area:	Gymnasium
Skills:	Overhand or underhand throwing, underhand rolling
Activity:	Designate one player as the toy soldier and the other as the toy maker. The toy maker stands on a marker at a specific distance from the toy soldier. The toy maker throws a ball to hit the soldier below chest level. If hit, the toy soldier begins marching in place, swinging the arms and legs. The toy maker then tries to turn off the toy soldier by throwing another ball. If hit, the toy turns off. If not hit, the toy remains on. The toy maker continues in this fashion turning the toy on and off. After a specific period of time, switch the toy soldier and toy maker, and repeat the activity.

Variations:
- Have various animals make different animal sounds when touched by a ball.
- Have the soldiers or animals move in a line and salute or turn around when hit with a ball.

Adaptations:
- Should the toy maker not be able to throw, use a ramp or mat for the ball to roll down.
- Place two toy soldiers or animals together if the target size needs to be larger.
- Designate animals that move slowly, such as a snail or a turtle, when animals are moving across. This will allow the players more time to throw or roll.
- Vary the distance that the toy maker and toy soldier stand apart to accommodate ability levels.

TRANSFORMER

Players:	Two per group (as many groups as needed)
Equipment:	Yarn balls
Area:	Gymnasium
Skills:	Overhand or underhand throwing
Activity:	Partners stand facing each other at specified distances. Designate one player as the "transformer", the other player as the "creator". The transformer begins by assuming a shape. The creator then attempts to change the shape of the toy by hitting it with yarn balls using underhand or overhand throwing. The transformer begins to move in place, making different shapes with every ball that touches it. The creator and transformer continue in this fashion until the toy is transformed completely. After a designated period of time, the two partners switch roles and repeat the process.
Variation:	• Allow the transformers to move around within a designated area; this increases the difficulty level by forcing the creator to throw at a moving target.
Adaptations:	• Depending on ability, vary the distance between partners.
	• Place two transformers side by side to increase the target size.

Colors

Players: Six to ten

Equipment: One playground ball

Area: Gymnasium or outside playing area

Skills: Underhand rolling, underhand throwing

Activity: One player stands in the middle of a circle of players. Each player chooses a different color. The player in the middle throws the playground ball in the air, simultaneously calling out a color. All players without that color, as well as the thrower, immediately run away from the circle. The player with the designated color must retrieve the ball and yell "Stop!" Everyone freezes on this command. The player with the ball then chooses someone as the target by rolling the ball toward this chosen player. If touched, that player becomes the thrower in the middle. If missed, the roller becomes the new thrower.

Variations: • Use the players' names if remembering colors becomes too confusing.

• Instead of running, use different locomotor skills such as skipping or galloping.

Adaptations: • Allow the players to take a specific number of steps or wheels toward the targeted person. Individualize numbers according to ability.

• Have students pair up and perform locomotor skills together as they move out from the circle. This then increases the target size for less-skilled rollers.

• If a student cannot roll very forcefully or accurately, allow that student to throw to the target or roll the ball down a ramp.

• When their name or color is called, players unable to catch or pick up the playground ball, can touch it with their hands, crutch tips, or wheelchair before yelling "Stop!"

OCTOPUS TAG

Players: Six or more

Equipment: Yarn balls

Area: Gymnasium or outside playing area

Skills: Locomotor skills, dodging, tagging, underhand rolling

Activity: The entire group lines up at one end of the playing area. One player is designated as the "octopus" and stands along the side of this area. Players attempt to cross the area to the other side without being tagged by the octopus. The octopus catches these "fish" by underhand rolling yarn balls to touch the fish. Any fish who is touched by a ball is caught and must remain frozen in that spot. All other fish move across and stop at the other end until the instructor directs them to run back. Stationary players then become "tentacles" of the octopus and attempt to tag other fish as they move by. Tentacles are not allowed to move from their spot to tag. They may only reach out to tag other players. The player's turn as the octopus ends when nearly all the fish are caught. Select another octopus, and repeat the activity.

Variations:
- Allow the octopus to overhand throw to catch fish.
- Have fish move across the playing area on scooters.

Adaptations:
- When lining up the players, position players so slower-moving fish are placed farther from the octopus while faster-moving fish are positioned closer.
- Vary the distance players must travel across to the safe area, depending upon the octopus's skill level and accuracy.
- Allow more than one octopus to roll if a student's skill level would prevent that player from catching many fish.

Puppy Dog Tails

Players:	Four or more
Equipment:	Long ropes (one for each player)
Area:	Gymnasium
Skills:	Locomotor skills, agility and body awareness, eye-foot coordination
Activity:	Randomly spread players out within the playing area. Each player has one end of a long rope tucked lightly into the back of their waistband or pocket. Stretch the other end onto the floor behind the player. Tell the players that they are puppies and that the ropes are the puppies' tails. Instruct them to move carefully around the playing area and to catch another puppy's tail by stepping on it, thus causing it to fall to the floor. Meanwhile, each puppy is also trying to avoid having its own tail caught. Once a puppy loses its tail, the puppy must jump over and back across the rope on the floor three times before picking it up and resuming play. Puppies are only allowed to catch another puppy's tail if both of their tails are still attached. You can use this activity after you have practiced other tag-type games with the players. Caution players to move carefully around the area; make sure they look ahead to where they are moving rather than back toward their tails.
Variation:	• Have horses with long tails gallop around the room.

Adaptations:
- Vary the locomotor movements, such as walking or skipping, to equalize the speed of play and individualize the game.
- Vary the length of the ropes; use shorter ropes for slow movers and longer ropes for fast movers.
- For movers who are nonambulatory, attach the rope to the back of the wheelchair (in back bag), and allow them shorter ropes if they maneuver more slowly.
- If the tail of a student using a wheelchair is caught, have the player wheel along the length of rope and follow its course before resuming play. Assist the student in picking up the rope and reattaching the tail.

ROLLING RED LIGHT

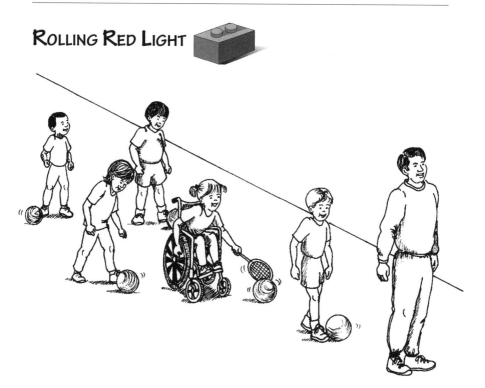

Players: Any number

Equipment: One playground ball per player

Area: Gymnasium or outside playing area

Skills: Kicking, soccer dribbling, soccer trapping

Activity: Players begin by standing side by side on one end of the playing area; each player has a ball. Stand on the opposite end of the area with your back toward the group. When you say "Green light!," each player begins dribbling the ball forward using the feet. When you call out "One, two, three, red light!," all players must quickly trap the ball and remain stationary. Quickly turn around to see if there are any players continuing to move or if any balls are still rolling. If a player or a ball is moving, that player must move two or three steps back and assume this new position. Players not caught moving remain in their space. The game continues in a similar fashion until one player reaches the end of the playing area where you are standing. This player then calls out the commands.

Variations: • Use different skills such as basketball dribbling or bouncing and catching.

- Have the student perform a certain skill related to the sport, such as three knee juggles with the soccer ball, instead of moving back two or three spaces.

Adaptations:
- Instead of soccer dribbling, have a student who is nonambulatory strike a foam ball using a long-handled racquet.

- Start less-skilled or slower-moving players closer to the instructor to equalize the time of the activity.

- Have less-skilled students take one step backward instead of two or three.

- Use various size balls.

- If trapping is difficult, allow some students to use their hands to stop the ball while still requiring them to dribble forward with their feet.

Steal the Bacon

Players: Six or more

Equipment: Two playground balls

Area: Gymnasium or outside playing area

Skills: Running, dodging, underhand throwing, catching

Activity: Divide the class evenly into two groups. Line up each group side by side, and have the two lines facing one another, approximately 20 feet apart. Place two playground balls in the center between the two groups. Give each member of a line a specific number so that both lines have players with corresponding numbers. After calling out a number, the two players with that number move to pick up one of the balls in the middle and bring it back to their respective team. The team members then throw the ball from one to the next, down the line. The player whose number was called runs around the team's line as many times as possible before the ball has reached the end of the line. Once the ball has reached the end of the line, the ball is given back to the player, and the player returns it to the middle. The player returning the ball to the middle first gets two points. A point is also awarded to each team for each lap completed. The game continues in this fashion as you call out different numbers.

Variations:
- Use different locomotor skills to retrieve the ball.
- Have a line perform different manipulative skills, such as a soccer pass, bounce pass, or over-and-under relay, to move the ball down the line.

Adaptations:
- For retrievers who are slower, require that the other team pass the ball up and down the line a specific number of times before giving it back and having it brought to the middle.
- For a player who is unable to catch while standing in line, have the ball rolled by the adjacent player.
- Match the players in terms of their speeds and abilities; assign them similar numbers.
- If one player is markedly slower, have the other player perform a specific number of exercises (jumping jacks or squat thrusts) before being able to move to the ball.

WHAT DO YOU LIKE TO EAT?

Players:	Four or more
Equipment:	Yarn balls and spot markers
Area:	Gymnasium
Skills:	Running, agility, overhand throwing
Activity:	Divide players into two groups. Position one group, side by side in a line, on one end of the area; scatter many yarn balls beside them. These players are the owls. Position the other group, the mice, on markers at a designated distance facing the owls who have their backs turned. When signaled to begin, the mice slowly and quietly make their way toward the owls. Ask, "What do you like to eat, Mr. and Mrs. Owl?" Owls may reply anything absurd, such as "Bananas," "Pizza," or "Cookies." When appropriate, interject and answer "MICE!" At this time, the mice turn and run toward their spots while the owls turn and begin throwing yarn balls to tag them. Owls may throw as many times and catch as many mice as they can before the mice reach safety. After a designated period of time, players change places and continue the game.
Variation:	• Have the owls actually turn and chase the mice to tag them before they reach safety.
Adaptations:	• Pair students by ability, and have the owl only throw to catch the particular mouse with whom that owl is paired. For example, pair fast runners with good throwers.
	• Utilize different animals or locomotor skills to equate speed and throwing ability. For example, have a fox catch rabbits who are attempting to jump back to their spots.
	• Depending upon speed of the mover and ability of the thrower, vary the distance that a particular mouse must travel to reach safety.

Duck Hunt

Players: Two or more

Equipment: Yarn balls, milk crates, and mats

Area: Gymnasium

Skills: Eye-hand coordination, overhand throwing, leg strength

Activity: Divide the players into two groups. Designate half of the students as ducks and have them begin in a line at one end of the area. Position the remaining students along the length of the area, parallel to where the ducks will be moving. The game begins when the ducks move across the area by stepping up onto and down from crates placed in a row, 2 to 3 feet apart. The duck hunters throw yarn balls in an attempt to hit the ducks. Ducks can only be hit when standing on top of a crate. If hit, the duck must step off the crate to the back and fall to the mat below. The duck then returns to the start of the row and begins to shuttle across again. If a duck is missed or hit when not on a crate, the duck continues moving forward to step on the next crate. Should a duck make it across the gallery without being caught, that duck returns to start again. Switch groups after a designated time so that all players have a chance to throw and shuttle. Make sure the ducks move at a constant speed and in the same direction. Ducks step up and down from crates only when moving from right to left. Otherwise, they shuttle back to the start behind this crate set-up.

Variation:
- Have frogs move across spot markers (lily pads); they may only be caught when not standing on a pad.

Adaptations:
- Use objects lower than crates if balance is a concern.
- Use more players if throwers need better opportunities to hit moving ducks or frogs.
- Make the game stationary by having the ducks stand on the perches rather than moving from perch to perch.
- For students who are nonambulatory or have motor difficulties, stack two crates for them to wheel or walk behind. Players sit or stand tall at appropriate intervals between the crates and bend forward or crouch down when behind crates.
- For individuals unable to throw, allow them to roll balls down a ramp and hit the crate itself. Ducks on the crates are caught when the crate is hit.
- Vary the distance between the crates, and allow more or less time for players to travel to the next crate.
- Vary the distance of the crates from the throwers.
- Vary the number of crates.

CROWS AND CRANES

Players:	Four or more
Equipment:	None
Area:	Gymnasium or outside playing area
Skills:	Running, tagging, agility, dodging
Activity:	Divide the group into two teams. Designate one team as crows and the other as cranes. Each group stands back to back on a line. If you call out "Crows!," the crows run to a predetermined line before the cranes can tag them. If you call "Cranes!," the cranes run to their line while the crows try to tag them. Once tagged, that individual joins the opposite team. Add to the anticipation by calling "Cr . . . cr . . . cr . . . cream!" or "Cr . . . cr . . .cr . . .crazy!"
Variation:	• Use the names of sport teams, such as Braves and Bruins.
Adaptations:	• Vary the distance specific players must move in order to be safe.
	• Have certain players perform an action, such as jumping jacks or toe touches, before being allowed to turn and chase another player.
	• Pair students by ability and place them on opposite sides. Allow these players to tag only their matched player.
	• Allow some students to throw yarn balls to tag.

FREEZE TAG . . . NOT!

Players:	Four or more
Equipment:	None
Area:	Gymnasium or outside playing area
Skills:	Locomotor skills, agility, tagging
Activity:	Designate one player as "it." Other players begin randomly moving throughout the area. The player who is "it" attempts to tag as many other players as possible in an allotted period of time. Players prevent themselves from being caught by freezing just before "it" touches them. Players can remain frozen for only three seconds. Otherwise, they must perform a designated skill to resume playing. Should a player be moving when tagged, that player must also perform a specific task in order to reenter the game. Choose a new "it," and resume play.
Variations:	• Vary the skills the players perform to reenter the game (e.g., sit-ups, jumping jacks, or hops).
	• Have more than one "it."
Adaptations:	• Pair one player who moves slowly with another who moves quickly; have both be "it" at the same time.
	• Vary the number of repetitions of a task in order for different players to reenter the game.
	• Depending upon the speed of the player who is "it," use different locomotor skills for the group.
	• Allow students in wheelchairs and those who may move slowly to throw yarn balls when attempting to tag others.
	• Vary the amount of time players can remain frozen. For example, designate a brief period of time that players can remain frozen for a slow "it."

Fill the Basket

Players:	Two or more
Equipment:	Yarn balls (at least one for every player) and one crate or box
Area:	Gymnasium
Skills:	Overhand throwing, catching
Activity:	Divide players into two groups, and position each group on one half of the playing area. Place a crate or box in the middle of the playing area on the line that separates the two groups. Players begin by overhand throwing yarn balls from their side of the playing area over to the players on the other side. The object is to throw the ball so that a player on the other side is able to catch it. A ball that is caught can then be placed into the crate in the middle. Any ball not caught in the air must be thrown back across the playing area to the players on the other side. The game continues in this cooperative manner until all the balls are caught and placed in the crate.
Variations:	• Use two crates, one for each team, and run the game in a competitive manner to see which group can fill its respective basket with more balls.

- Time the class, and have the players attempt to beat their best time.

Adaptations: • For those students unable to catch thrown balls, have other students roll the balls across the gym to them. Balls must be caught before they stop rolling.

- Use a few, larger balls (beach balls or foam balls) designated for specific students to catch.

- For those students using wheelchairs, have some balls placed in their laps for them to throw. Allow these students to move and touch the ball with their wheelchairs to "catch" it before the ball stops moving.

MARBLES

Players:	8 to 10 per circle (as many circles as needed)
Equipment:	Tape or white shoe polish, 12 to 15 foam balls (3 inches in diameter), and yarn balls
Area:	Gymnasium
Skills:	Underhand rolling, eye-hand coordination
Activity:	Tape a large circle on the floor or use white shoe polish to mark the area. Within the circle, scatter all the "marbles" (foam balls). Players stand around the circle, 8 to 10 feet away. Give each player six to eight yarn balls to begin. Players underhand roll the yarn balls toward the circle, attempting to hit the foam balls and to move them outside the circle. Players retrieve the yarn balls rolled across, but they must return to their original spot before attempting another underhand roll. The game ends when all the foam balls have been moved outside the circle.
Variations:	• Time the group, and have them try to beat their best time.

- Use two circles and two groups; run the game competitively by having each group race to clear its own circle first.

Adaptations:
- If the students are unable to roll forcefully enough to move the foam balls, use fully inflated beach balls as the marbles.

- If the students are unable to underhand roll, use a wedge bolster or ramp for the students to roll the balls down.

- Vary the distances the students stand from the circle based on individual abilities. If using two groups, vary the number of balls in each circle to equalize the time to complete the game.

PONIES IN THE BARN

Players:	Six or more
Equipment:	Spot markers and yarn balls
Area:	Gymnasium
Skills:	Overhand throwing, galloping, agility
Activity:	Place spot markers in a large circle. All players, except one, take a position on one of the "barns" (markers). The player in the middle initiates the game by saying, "Run, ponies, run!" All the players gallop to another barn. The player in the center then attempts to catch a "pony" by throwing a yarn ball and touching the pony while it is outside a barn. Ponies cannot be captured while standing in a barn. Once a pony is captured, the pony must gallop around the outside of the barns one time before reentering the game.
Variation:	• Have different animals move from barn to barn using various locomotor skills or animal walks.

Adaptations: • For skilled throwers, increase the number of barns to decrease the amount of time ponies travel from one barn to the next.

• For less-skilled throwers, decrease the number of barns to increase the time during which the ponies can be caught.

• Pair a lesser-skilled thrower with a higher-skilled thrower; place them in the center together, and have both capture ponies simultaneously.

• Allow slower movers to be touched two times with the balls before being caught.

ROLL OVER

Players:	Four or more
Equipment:	One large, plastic therapy ball; yarn balls; and 18 inch by 24 inch floor targets with numbers
Area:	Gymnasium
Skills:	Overhand throwing, underhand throwing
Activity:	Mark a square playing area (the size depends upon the number of players). Scatter numbered floor targets randomly throughout the designated playing area. Evenly divide players into four groups, and make each group responsible for one side of the square. Players throw yarn balls at the plastic therapy ball in order to move it toward and over the specified, numbered targets. Players cooperatively move the ball by throwing at it to achieve the desired direction. The group attempts to move the target ball over the numbers in sequential order.
Variation:	• Have the group move the target ball over the targets, attempting to get as many points as possible within a designated time period.
Adaptations:	• Have students with less throwing ability and arm strength positioned next to the players with higher skill levels.

- Have one or two floor targets positioned close to students with less throwing ability.
- Allow students with decreased arm strength to use heavier balls (playground balls) and to roll the ball down a ramp.
- Use targets of various sizes based on the ability levels of the players.

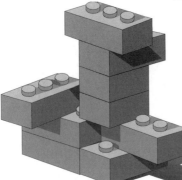

CHAPTER 4

ADVANCED
ACTIVITIES

Centipede

Players:　　　Four or more

Equipment:　Beanbags, yarn balls, and cones

Area:　　　　Gymnasium

Skills:　　　　Overhand throwing, running, dodging

Activity:　　　Line up all players, except for one, at one end of the playing area. The player to be the centipede begins at the opposite end of the area with 15 beanbags. Set up a zigzag, slalom-like course using cones spaced 20 to 25 feet apart. The object of the game is for the centipede to make it through the course to the last cone, attempting to keep as many of the body segments (beanbags) as possible. The other players overhand throw yarn balls at the centipede, trying to hit it with the balls. Each time a ball touches the centipede, it must drop one of its body parts (beanbags). Once the centipede finishes, its remaining body parts are counted and a new centipede is chosen. Repeat the game until all have had a chance to be the centipede.

Variations:　　• Have more than one centipede moving at a time.

　　　　　　　　• Vary the skill used to hit the centipede; try underhand rolling or striking.

　　　　　　　　• Vary the course the centipede must travel.

Adaptations:
- Vary the number of body parts for each centipede, taking speed and agility levels into account.
- Allow less distance between cones for slower movers.
- Vary the distance players must throw in order to reach the centipede.

Mission Possible

Players: Three to seven per group (as many groups as needed)

Equipment: One playground ball per group and tape for marking goals on the wall

Area: Gymnasium

Skills: Soccer passing, trapping, shooting on goal

Activity: Choose one player from each group to be the offensive player who will shoot on goal. This player attempts to repeatedly kick the ball to the wall between the taped goal marks (2 feet wide), trapping the ball between each kick. This player tries to make as many goals as possible before the rest of the group yells "Stop!" Position the other players in a circle. They begin by passing the ball, using an inside-of-the-foot pass, across the circle to another player who traps the ball before passing it to another player. The ball does not need to be passed in any particular order, but all players in the circle must pass and trap at least one time. The group passes and traps the ball 10 times before shouting "Stop!" At this point, all the offensive players stop and add up their total goals. A new offensive player from each group is then selected. Play continues in this fashion until all have had a chance to shoot on goal. Add up the points of the various teams (groups of offensive players), and compare scores.

Variations: • Utilize different skills, such as dribbling, bounce passes, striking, or throwing and catching.

• Have two players pass between one another in order to get points (the total number of passes completed before the group stops them).

Adaptations: • Vary the number of passes a group must make in accordance with the ability level of the offensive player.

• Have the players kick at the goal one at a time rather than using repetitive kicks; provide assistance for returning the ball to the student, if necessary.

• Use striking instead of kicking if the student is nonambulatory.

• Use larger balls.

- Allow students who are unable to trap with their feet to use their hands to stop the ball before making a pass. Otherwise, provide support to the player's hand if trapping is unlikely due to balance difficulties.

PIN BALL

Players: Two or more

Equipment: Yarn balls and plastic bowling pins

Area: Gymnasium

Skill: Overhand throwing

Activity: Divide the group into two teams. Line up each team side by side, opposite one another and separated by a distance of 20 feet. Place a row of plastic bowling pins just ahead of each team. The object of the game is for each team to throw their yarn balls and to knock over the other team's pins before their own pins are knocked down.

Variations: • Number the pins, and require teams to knock down pins in sequence.

• Have only one set of pins that both groups try to knock over; work cooperatively to achieve the best time.

Adaptations: • Place the pins closer or farther apart, depending upon the throwing ability of students.

• Place pairs of pins together to make larger targets.

- Position pins in a diagonal to allow one end to be at a closer distance to the less-skilled throwers.
- Use a ramp for those unable to throw.
- Alter the number of pins each team has, depending upon the team's speed and throwing accuracy.

THE GIANT'S GUM BALL

Players: 10 to 12 per group

Equipment: One large earthball

Area: Gymnasium or outside playing area

Skills: Cooperation, teamwork

Activity: The objective is for the group to move the giant's gum ball, without letting it touch the ground, from one end of the playing area to a specific destination ahead (the distance depends on the size of the group). When moving the ball, no player can stand, at least two players must touch the ball at all times, and every player must assist in passing the ball at some time. The group begins in a line. The ball is passed (using hands, legs, or stomachs) from one player to the next. As the ball nears the end of the line, players from the beginning move to a position ahead of the ball and are ready to continue the ball's motion. This process continues until the ball reaches the designated location. The group must begin again if they do not successfully fulfill the criteria.

Variations: • Have two balls moving simultaneously.

                 • Require the players to use only their feet and legs.

- If there is a large group, require more people to touch the ball simultaneously, and increase the distance the ball needs to travel.

Adaptations:
- Allow a student using a wheelchair to remain in the chair and to use it to support the ball, if necessary.
- Use a lightweight therapy ball if the entire group's ability warrants it.
- Change the distance the ball needs to travel according to the group's ability and mobility levels.

Happy Landings

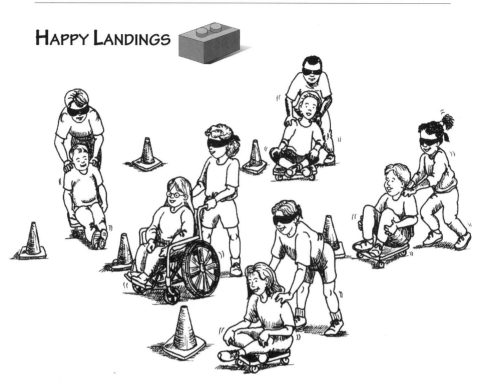

Players: Two per group (as many groups as necessary and as space allows)

Equipment: Blindfolds, one scooter per group, 10 to 12 cones, and miscellaneous equipment

Area: Gymnasium

Skills: Communication, cooperation, trust

Activity: Pair players, and position them at one end of the gym. The two will attempt to maneuver their boat (scooter) through a rock-strewn channel (cones and miscellaneous equipment) and land safely by the dock at the other end. The two crew members are survivors of a large ship that exploded. Unfortunately, one member was blinded in the explosion, and the other was wounded seriously in the legs; both did, however, escape in a small rowboat. The injured crew member sits in the boat with the blinded partner behind. The two members begin their quest for survival; the sighted player provides verbal directions for the blindfolded partner to pull or push the scooter. The sighted player must give clear directions so as not to cause the boat to hit any rocks or obstacles. When the boat has docked safely on the other end of the channel, the two switch places and roles. Rocks and obstacles are re-arranged in the water. If there is a large class, some students may serve as rocks or obstacles in the channel.

Variations:
- Have the blindfolded rower move according to a dock worker's directions (given from the other end of the playing area).

- Use specific signals instead of words to direct the boat.

Adaptations:
- Put power wheelchairs in manual mode so that they can be pushed by the partners.

- Ensure that individuals using communication devices have the ability to give directional commands and signals.

- Have a student in a wheelchair pull the partner who is sitting on the scooter; use a rope to attach the scooter to the wheelchair. Remind the student to drive slowly and carefully because the scooter may swerve and may not roll in a straight line. Allow enough space between the rocks to account for this extra movement.

Krazy Kickball

Players:	10 to 12 per team
Equipment:	One playground ball and four bases
Area:	Gymnasium or outside playing area
Skills:	Kicking, base running, passing
Activity:	Divide the group into two teams. The object is for the kicker on one team to kick the ball and run around the bases as many times as possible before the team in the field stops the kicker. The ball can be kicked in any direction within bounds. The fielders are scattered throughout the playing area until the ball is kicked. After the kick, they quickly form a line behind the person who retrieved the ball and pass it over and under to the last person in line, who then yells "Stop!" The fielding team attempts to pass the ball to this last person as fast as possible in order to stop the kicker from moving around the bases. One point is scored for each base touched by the kicker. After everyone has kicked on one team, all the points are added together, and the teams change sides. Repeat the process with the new kicking team.
Variations:	• Utilize other skills, such as throwing, dribbling, or striking, instead of kicking.
	• Have fielders bounce pass, soccer pass, or throw and catch to one another until all have touched the ball.
Adaptations:	• Vary the distance between the bases, depending upon the runner's speed.
	• Have fielders pass the ball more than one time down the line. Designate a specific number for various players in order to account for differences in speed.
	• Have the player kick a rolling ball or a stationary one, depending upon ability.
	• Use different size balls, if necessary.
	• Have fielders roll the ball to one another if catching skills are not well-developed.

Square Off

Players:	Four or more
Equipment:	Yarn balls, large beach ball or plastic therapy ball, and four cones
Area:	Gymnasium
Skills:	Overhand throwing, eye-hand coordination
Activity:	Outline a large square using four cones at the corners. Divide players evenly into four groups. Each group positions itself along one side of the square. Place the target ball (the large beach ball or plastic therapy ball) in the center of the square. On your command, the players begin throwing yarn balls at the target ball. The objective is for each group to move the target ball toward their opponents and over one of the three other sides of the square outlined by the cones. Players can move along the length of their own side but cannot move to another side of the square or touch the target ball with any parts of their bodies.
Variations:	• Have two sides team up and work together to move the target ball across the opposing teams' lines.
	• Have the four groups work cooperatively to move the target ball in specified patterns on the floor.
Adaptations:	• Allow players who are unable to throw to use ramps to roll the balls. Assistance may be necessary to position the ramps.
	• Assure that all groups have evenly distributed ability levels.
	• Use a larger target ball.
	• Vary the size of the groups on each side, taking ability levels into account.
	• Vary the length of goal lines. You do not need to use a perfect square.

STRIKE BACK

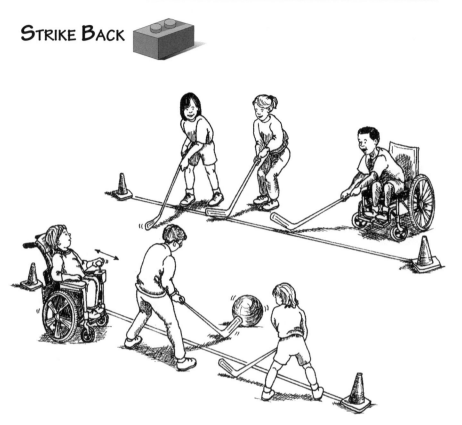

Players: Four or more

Equipment: Floor hockey sticks, 8-inch foam ball, and four cones

Area: Gymnasium

Skills: Forehand striking, backhand striking

Activity: Divide players into two teams. Position each team on a goal line between two cones. Assure that 1 to 2 feet of space exists between the players and between the players and the end cones. Each team tries to strike the ball across the opponent's goal line. Each team, in turn, also tries to prevent the goal and immediately strikes the ball back. The ball must remain on the ground at all times, and sticks must stay below waist level. Encourage players to pass the ball down the line to others on the same team before shooting across the playing area. A goal is scored every time the ball crosses the goal line. The game continues in this fashion for a designated period of time.

Variations: • Have the two goals at either end of the playing area, and place the players from both teams alternately on the sides.

• Use colored shirts to distinguish players and to denote the appropriate goal.

Adaptations: • Position players with only the ability to forehand or backhand strike next to teammates with more mobility and function.

• Allow players using power wheelchairs to move forward and backward along the line and to use the sides of their wheelchairs to block balls.

• Use nylon racquets attached to hockey sticks or to longer handles for those who need an increased striking surface.

• Vary the distance between the two teams, depending upon ability levels.

• Vary the size and type of the ball for slow- or fast-paced games.

• Use a slightly deflated beach ball to reduce resiliency and decrease speed.

Across the Great Divide

Players:	Six or more
Equipment:	None
Area:	Gymnasium or outside playing area
Skills:	Cooperation, communication, teamwork
Activity:	Line up the group side by side, all facing the same direction. Instruct the players to position their feet so that the outside of each foot touches the outside of the foot of the person standing to either side. Explain the following scenario to the group: "Way back, when settlers arrived, they had to prove that they could work together and that they were worthy of the land. In order to be given the deed to the land, the group had to move from one point to another without breaking contact." The group then tries to move the designated distance while keeping their feet in contact. Should anyone in the line lose contact, the group must return to the start and begin again.
Variation:	• If the group is advanced enough, blindfold some members of the group during the activity.

Adaptations: • Vary the distance that the group needs to move, depending on the group's ability and its prior experience with cooperative games.

• Position a student using a wheelchair on one end. Use a velcro band to connect the foot rest of the wheelchair to the ankle or knee of the ambulatory person standing beside it. Allow enough space in the band to allow the ambulatory member's foot to contact the ground but not get injured by the wheelchair; the two members need to remain close enough to force them to work together.

Gym Invaders

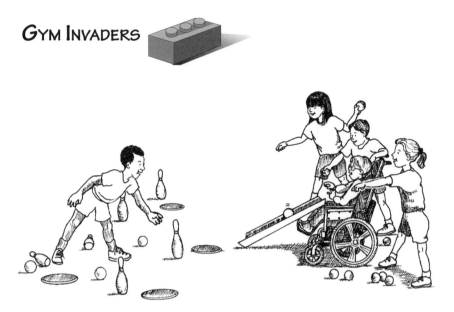

Players:	Two or more
Equipment:	Yarn balls, plastic bowling pins, and spot markers
Area:	Gymnasium
Skills:	Throwing, running, dodging
Activity:	Before beginning, randomly place bowling pins in the playing area. Choose one person to start as the gym invader. This player attempts to run and knock down as many pins as possible with the hands. The others in the group try to stop the gym invader by throwing yarn balls to hit the invader from specified distances designated by the spot markers. Throwers try to blow up the gym invader to end the player's turn. The invader tries to dodge the thrown balls while knocking over the pins. Throwers may also try to knock down pins to prevent the gym invader from reaching them. The gym invader receives one point for each pin knocked down, excluding those knocked over by thrown balls. After the gym invader has been blown up (touched) five times, a new player becomes the gym invader.
Variations:	• Place cardboard bricks in the playing area; these will be worth more points if knocked over.
	• Place spot markers in the playing area that act as gym mines and blow up the invader if touched.

                               • Add crates to provide shelter behind which the gym invader can hide.

Adaptations: • If the players are unable to throw, have them roll the balls down mats or ramps.

                               • Modify the distance players must throw to hit the gym invader.

                               • Vary the spaces between the pins, depending upon the speed of the gym invader. If a player is very fast, make the spaces large. If a player is slow, make the spaces smaller, and give each player an equal chance to knock over the same number of pins.

                               • Vary the number of blow-ups allowed for each gym invader according to that player's speed.

HOME PLATE BASEBALL

Players: 8 to 10 per team

Equipment: Bats, softball, four bases, and t-stand

Area: Gymnasium or outside playing area

Skills: Batting, running, fielding, catching, throwing

Activity: Divide the group into two teams. One team is the fielding team and is positioned out in the field as in regulation baseball. The members of the batting team bat one at a time. A batter gets three pitched balls before having to use the batting tee. The batter hits the ball and begins to move around the bases without stopping. The fielders must field the batted ball and throw it to the instructor standing near the pitcher's mound. The instructor must then bring the thrown ball to home base in order to stop the batter from running. The batter receives one point for each base touched before the ball is brought to home plate. Each batter on the team bats, and all points are added together. Teams switch places and repeat the activity.

Variations: • Use just two bases, one across from the other. The batter shuttles between the bases.

• Have runner decide whether or not to advance to the next base, depending upon how fast the fielders can get the ball home. The instructor receiving the fielded ball tries to reach the appropriate base first.

Adaptations: • Vary the distance bases are placed apart, based on the speed of individual players.

• Allow outfielders in wheelchairs to have an additional ball on their laps. After moving to touch the batted ball with the chair, the player throws the ball on the lap to home plate.

• Ensure that the instructor moves out to an appropriate distance from the fielder to receive the ball.

• For slower moving batters or those that cannot hit the ball very far, have the fielders throw the ball a specific number of times among themselves before throwing it to home plate.

Poison Peanut Butter Pit

Players:	Eight or more
Equipment:	A large plastic or canvas tarp
Area:	Gymnasium or outside playing area
Skills:	Cooperation, communication, teamwork
Activity:	The group begins by standing on a large tarp. The tarp must be large enough for the group to move freely from one side to the other. Explain the following scenario to the group: "Just recently, there was an earthquake in the area. The tremors were so violent that the peanut butter factory and the chemical company were leveled to the ground. As a result, poison peanut butter covered the entire area, leaving the company workers stranded on a chemical-resistant tarp left in the warehouse. The group must somehow move to a rescue vehicle waiting across the road." The group then attempts to move across the pit while remaining on the tarp and not touching any of the poisonous peanut butter (the area around the tarp). Players must remain on the tarp the entire width of the pit (designated distance) in order to reach safety on the other side. Allow the group time to solve the problem and discuss possible solutions. One possible solution is: The group shifts to one side of the tarp, folds the tarp over in the middle, moves across to a smaller section, unfolds the tarp, and slides it out in the opposite direction.
Variations:	• Place obstacles within the pit; the group must avoid the obstacles to remain safe. • Place two groups on two tarps, and see if other solutions arise.
Adaptation:	• Adjust the size of the pit to accommodate the group's ability and mobility levels. Because this can be a long process in the initial stages, begin with a reduced distance.

THE TORTOISE AND THE HARE

Players: Six or more

Equipment: Blindfolds and cones

Area: Gymnasium or outside playing area

Skills: Communication, cooperation, trust

Activity: Choose two members of the group to begin the activity; designate one as the tortoise and the other as the hare. Each player will attempt to move through the forest without falling into any snares previously set up by poachers. Unfortunately, the snares are well hidden and impossible for the two to see (the two players are blind-folded). A few players are randomly scattered in the forest area and act as snares. These snares must remain station-ary and use only their arms to catch the animals. (Cones may also be used as snares.) The remaining players are divided into two groups. These individuals will serve as the rangers who protect the animals within the forest. One-half of the group will line the area on one side and verbally guide the tortoise to safety, while the other half of the group will line up on the opposite side and verbally guide the hare to safety. Each group will guide its respective animal through the forest to the clearing at the other side. When the animals reach safety, choose two new members. Should an animal be caught in a snare, that player must begin again.

Variations:
- Have the players direct more than two animals through the forest at the same time.

- Have one group try to guide a fox to catch the rabbit that the other group is directing.

Adaptations:
- Ensure that the players do not run into any students using wheelchairs, and vice-versa, by using an emergency stop signal.

- Allow larger spaces in between snares.

- Attempt to equalize the two moving animals by pairing members according to their speed.

CHAPTER 5

ADAPTED SPORT ACTIVITIES

The presentation of activities in this chapter differs from that of previous chapters. The activities offered here are sport activities. There are no theme variations, and specific adaptations are incorporated directly into the description of the sport itself. The adapted sport may be used, as described, for an entire group needing such modifications, or specific components outlined may be used for a particular individual within an inclusive situation. Volleyball, however, serves more as an adapted sport than an inclusive activity because of the nature of the game and the use of only one ball.

These are just a few of the many modifications that can be used for adapting sport activities. Specific adaptations will ultimately depend on the nature of the group and ability levels of the individuals within the game.

TABLE TENNIS

Players: Two to four per table

Equipment: Paddles or nylon racquets, whiffle balls, and wooden rails

Area: Gymnasium

Skills: Forehand striking, backhand striking

Activity: Clamp wooden rails around both sides of a regulation table to prevent the ball from rolling off the table. Do not use a net. Pair players who are unable to externally rotate their arms with a mobile player for doubles. Position the team so that the player with limited range of motion can play using a backhand. Players strike the ball so that it rolls across the length of the table to the opposite end. The object is for each player or team to prevent the ball from rolling off its own end of the table. A point is scored if the opponent hits the ball over the side borders or allows the ball to roll off their end of the table. Some players may be allowed to hit the ball more than one time. Scoring is the same as in a regulation game. Vary the type of ball (whiffle balls or Ping-Pong balls) or type of racquet (Ping-Pong paddles or nylon racquets), depending upon the ability of the players.

BASEBALL

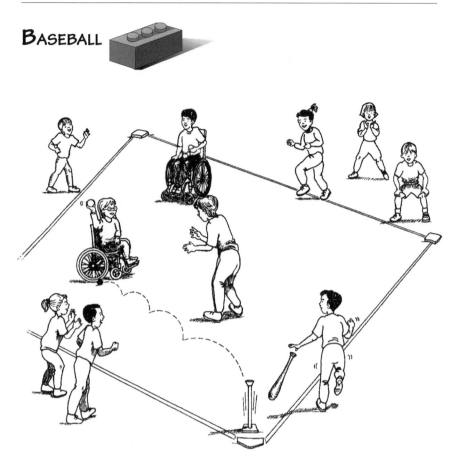

Players: 8 to 10 per team

Equipment: T-stand, bats, whiffle balls, four bases, yarn balls, and ramp

Area: Gymnasium or outside playing area

Skills: Batting, base running, fielding, throwing

Activity: Divide the group into two teams. The batting team bats one at a time using a t-stand, t-stand with ramp (for those players with limited ability to hit the ball with either a bat or their hand), or a pitched ball. The batter hits the ball and moves around the bases as in a regulation game. Position the fielding team outside the base path, and spread far enough apart to cover the entire area. The fielder closest to the ball fields it according to his or her abilities. An ambulatory fielder retrieves the ball and brings it to the appropriate base or throws it to the instructor who is standing in the center of the field. Fielders who are nonambulatory have yarn balls in their laps. They field the ball by positioning their wheelchairs so that the hit ball touches the chair. Once the hit ball is touched, the fielder throws the yarn ball from their laps to the instructor. The instructor must catch the ball and move to the appropriate base. If the batter reaches the base before the fielded ball, the batter is safe. If the fielded ball reaches the base before the batter, the batter is out. The game continues in a similar fashion, and the teams exchange places after every three outs. Scoring is the same as in a regulation game.

Football

Players: Six or more

Equipment: Footballs of various sizes, yarn balls

Area: Gymnasium or outside playing area

Skills: Maneuvering, throwing, catching, agility

Activity: Divide the group into two teams with an even number of players on each team. The offensive team chooses a center, a quarterback, and two to four receivers. Assign defensive players to cover offensive players of equal ability. Defense has one-on-one coverage on all receivers as well as a rusher. The rusher must first count out loud to a specified number, depending on the rusher's ability and quickness, and then move to tag the quarterback before the quarterback releases the football. If the rusher is unable to tag, a yarn ball can be thrown or dropped to the floor to "sack" the quarterback. The quarterback uses a multicolored yarn ball, Nerf football, or mini-football, depending upon grasping ability. A complete pass is one that is caught by a designated receiver. For those players unable to catch, a complete pass is one that touches this player's body or wheelchair. Once the pass is caught or touched, the receiver moves toward the goal. A defensive player attempts to stop the receiver from scoring by first following the offensive player and then tagging the player by hand or by throwing a yarn ball from the lap. (This prevents potential collisions between wheelchairs.) The offense has four downs to score. There are no interceptions. After four downs, the defensive team takes over the ball wherever the offense was stopped. Scoring is the same as in a regulation game, except there are no extra-point plays.

VOLLEYBALL

Players: Eight or more

Equipment: One large balloon or beach ball, a net

Area: Gymnasium

Skills: Serving, setting, bumping, volleying

Activity: Divide the group into two teams. Position each team on one side of a lowered net; place the higher-skilled, mobile players in the back and the less-skilled, stationary players toward the front. Players remain in these positions and do not rotate during the game. The game begins when one player serves the ball over the net, and players attempt to return the ball over the net. The game continues the same as in a regulation match. The teams are, however, allowed to hit the ball as many times as needed to get it back over to the other side. Points may also be awarded to players who use the correct skill (bump or set shot) and for ensuring three hits per side. Otherwise, the game follows the regular serving and scoring guidelines.

GLOSSARY OF MOVEMENTS AND POSITIONS

Body awareness: awareness, identification, and evaluation of the positions and movements of one's own body and/or body parts.

Crab walk: walking on hands and feet with stomach face up and buttocks off floor.

Crawling: movement of the body while lying on the floor.

Creeping: movement of the body while on hands and knees.

Crossing midline: ability to perform tasks requiring that the eyes or extremities cross the theoretical line that vertically divides the body into two equal halves.

Four-point stance: assuming a hands and knees position with stomach off floor.

Half-kneel: stationary position with one knee and sole of other foot on floor, trunk and head upright.

Kneeling balance: maintaining stability while in a stationary position on knees.

Knee walking: locomotion by alternating movement of the legs while in a kneeling position.

Locomotor skills: movements that transport the body from one space to another; traveling.

Manipulative skills: actions in which the body sends, receives, and maintains possession of objects.

Motor planning: sequencing of skills or movements in a meaningful manner.

Prone on elbows: on stomach with upper chest and head elevated and supported by elbows.

Range of motion: the possible motion available at a specific joint.

Seal walk: walking on hands while dragging stomach and legs on floor.

Soccer trap: a soccer skill aimed at receiving the ball where the foot is angled up with the heel down, and the sole of the foot is used to stop and control the ball.

Wheelchair push-up: lifting of the buttocks off seat by pushing up with hands and arms from arm rests.

SUGGESTED READINGS

Inspiration for some of the games found throughout *Inclusive Games* came from a number of sources. The following books are great resources; they detail games and activities that are appropriate for, or can be modified to include, children of all abilities.

Lichtman, B. (1993). *Innovative games.* Champaign, IL: Human Kinetics.

Morris, G.S., & Stiehl, J. (1989). *Changing kid's games.* Champaign, IL: Human Kinetics.

Pangrazi, R.P. & Dauer, V.P., (1994). *Dynamic physical education for elementary school children* (11th ed.). New York: Macmillan.

Poppen, J.D., & Jacobson, S.A. (1982). *Games that come alive.* Puyallup, WA: Action Productions.

ABOUT THE AUTHOR

After receiving her master's degree in special physical education from the University of Wisconsin-La Crosse, Susan Kasser taught children ages 3 to 15 both adapted and integrated physical education from 1984 to 1993. She developed many games to meet the unique abilities and needs of her students, and she implemented an adapted sports program that greatly improved the skill levels of the children.

Susan was a member of a CHOICES (Children Have Opportunities in Integrated Community Environments) grant committee, emphasizing inclusive education programs. She also received a Certificate of Recognition from the Illinois Coalition of School Professors and University Programs in Adapted Physical Education.

Susan, a faculty member in the Department of Exercise and Sport Science at Oregon State University, conducts numerous conference workshops to help physical education teachers learn to adapt games to include students of all skill levels. She is a member of the American Alliance of Health, Physical Education, Recreation and Dance and of the National Consortium for Physical Education and Recreation for Individuals with Disabilities.

A native of Massachusetts, Susan lives in Corvallis, Oregon. In her spare time she enjoys jogging, canoeing, hiking, and backpacking.

More HK books on children and physical activity

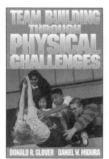